THAT SWEET CITY

And that sweet city with her dreaming spires,
She needs not June for beauty's heightening.
Matthew Arnold, *Thyrsis*

THAT SWEET CITY
Visions of Oxford

Poems by JOHN ELINGER
Illustrations by KATHERINE SHOCK

SIGNAL BOOKS

Oxford

First published in 2013 by
Signal Books Limited
36 Minster Road
Oxford
OX4 1LY
www.signalbooks.co.uk

A catalogue record for this book is available
from the British Library.

ISBN 978–1–908493–78–1 Paper

Production: Baseline Arts Ltd
Cover Design: Baseline Arts Ltd
Cover Images: Katherine Shock
Illustrations: Katherine Shock
Printed in India

CONTENTS

INTRODUCTION

I. OXFORD TODAY

On May Day madcap students leap
from Magdalen Bridge – and hurt themselves.
The streets are full of litter. Cheap
trinkets for tourists fill the shelves
of shops in Oxford – where it's rare,
when summer comes, to hear a word
of English! Then St. Giles's Fair
disturbs the peace. Old people herd
at bus-stops in the rain. New Year
gives more excuse for drunkenness
and swearing, casual sex and beer –
all seven sins in decadent excess.

But look a little deeper, listen
more closely, you will hear the bells
at Michaelmas and see dew glisten
in Christ Church Meadows. What compels
lasting attention isn't getting
and spending, envy, greed and lust –
but hearing birdsong, watching setting
suns, snowfalls, trees in leaf, or just
noticing winter's stars explode
(to make new worlds one day?),
the blossom on the Banbury Road
and Magdalen's fritillaries in May.

THE POEM SEEKS TO CAPTURE the superficial and occasional ugliness, and the deep enduring beauty, of Oxford today. What are the facts? Oxford, the County Town of Oxfordshire, lies in the centre of the south of England, almost equidistant between Bristol and London (to the west and east) and Birmingham and Southampton (to the north and south). Traffic permitting, it has good connections in all directions, by road, by railway, along the River Thames to the east and the Oxford Canal to the north. It even boasts its own little airport at nearby Kidlington. Local buses are frequent and generally reliable. Long-distance buses and coaches carry travellers to all points of the compass; there is an excellent – and inexpensive – coach service to central London (two, in fact) about fifty miles away.

The City is encircled by a well-preserved green belt and an arc of low limestone hills to the south. It sits on a sort of gravel terrace above and beside the two rivers, the Cherwell and the Thames, which meet at Oxford. The climate is temperate, the land low-lying (only two hundred feet above sea level), the weather variable, the temperature moderate. Apart from occasional minor flooding from the rivers, nature's more extreme conditions are almost unknown here.

[2]

Almost 165,000 people live in Oxford. It is a cosmopolitan population, with roughly thirty per cent being relatively recent immigrants to the UK – of whom about a half represent the visible ethnic minorities. What do they do? In the past, apart from its famous University, Oxford was known for its beer and marmalade. The City's major industries today are: education and research, publishing and book-selling, health, tourism, motor manufacture, and new IT and science-based businesses located in the Science and Business Parks to the east. Oxford is a curious hybrid of a somewhat decayed south-midland manufacturing town across Magdalen Bridge in the Cowley area, where the motor works extends over many acres and is a major employer, new hi-tech business start-ups, and the historic centre of learning – with two universities, a major teaching hospital, and a remarkable and diverse collection of colleges and schools, attracting over 50,000 students and nearly ten million tourists every year.

They come to admire the old buildings, learn something of the remarkable history, share the lively culture, and visit the busy shopping centres, of this unique City. They are not disappointed. Oxford has something for everyone. The sights of this 'sweet city' deserve to be numbered among the wonders of the world.

2. THE HISTORY OF OXFORD

Cities survive in story: buildings rise
and fall, stone crumbles, fashions change, and time
transforms the tallest towers to dust, sublime
structures to ash; but, when a city dies,
its history lives on to please, surprise,
inform another generation. Rhyme
preserves the past – and images may prime
enquiring minds, and make the studious wise.

The history of Oxford is a tale
worth telling – rivalry of Town and Gown,
of Church and Monarch, Parliament and Crown,
of science and religion, thought and things ...
A city's story changes – never stale,
whatever challenges the future brings.

[3]

AS THE POEM SUGGESTS, Oxford's history is one of conflict between contending powers or forces, interests or ideas. Often, its local story reflects national or even European struggles. The history of Oxford echoes and highlights the history of England.

Understanding the past often requires the disentangling of history from legend. Oxford is no exception to this rule. We can, for example, discount the story that University College – and the University of Oxford itself – were founded by King Alfred, and must doubt the dramatic legend of St. Frideswide, who miraculously restored the sight of the man who had pursued her and been struck blind for his wickedness. Even the two or three coins issued by a certain (untitled) Alfred at 'Ohsnaforda' do not clearly prove the existence of a significant settlement much before the end of the ninth century.

Oxford enters recorded history at the beginning of the tenth century, when the Anglo-Saxon Chronicle for 912 reports that 'King Edward [son of Alfred the Great] took possession of London and Oxford and all the land belonging with them'. The name of the City is Anglo-Saxon: 'a ford for cattle' (across the Thames). And the earliest surviving building can be dated to about 1000: the Saxon tower of St. Michael-at-the-Northgate (in the Cornmarket).

While there are a few traces of Roman settlements, and earlier Saxon burials in the Oxford area, the town seems to have come into being during the later ninth century. But then it grew rapidly both in size and importance. Its location on the border between Wessex and Mercia, and later between Anglo-Saxon England and the Danelaw, defined by the River Thames, made it a strategic priority for the defence of the Saxon south of the country.

It was also an important trading centre, conveniently located on the intersection of roads linking the north and south, and the east and west, of England. Carfax, the crossroads at the City centre, is a Norman French word derived from Latin *quadrifurcus*, 'four-forked'. The ford, possibly located at North Hinksey, but more probably south of the City near the end of St. Aldate's (earlier Fish Street), and the earliest bridge which replaced it, made Oxford a gateway between the north and south.

The Norman Conquest of 1066 changed everything – and transformed Oxford. Once for all, England was united under a powerful leader, William I. The Norman rulers governed England ruthlessly and effectively. They built castles as strongholds and demonstrations of power; they transferred the ownership of land by sequestration from the Saxon landowners and grants to the Norman invaders – this high-handed act was given a veil of legitimacy in the Domesday Book (1086); and they imposed their language and culture on the English. Only in the case of the language were they ultimately unsuccessful, though Modern English contains a large number of French words from this period and later.

The Norman governor of Oxford, Robert D'Oyly, built the castle outside the West Gate of the City, where it has survived to this day, first as a prison, now an upmarket hotel. The original structure was apparently a wooden tower on the top of the mound. Examples of Norman architecture in Oxford are found in the church of St. Peter-in-the-East (now the library of St. Edmund Hall), the old monastic church of St. Frideswide (now the Cathedral of Oxford and chapel of Christ Church), and Iffley Church, which lies a mile to the south of the City by the Thames.

Oxford, which had some 1,000 homes and eleven churches in 1066, is described in the Domesday Book as a place in decline. Over half the houses were in ruins. But it soon revived, and was frequently visited by successive monarchs who liked to stay in Beaumont Palace (surviving only in a street name), built – near the Ashmolean Museum's location today – by Henry I at the beginning of the twelfth century. Richard I was born there in 1137. Henry's daughter, the Empress Maud, was residing in the Castle when Oxford was besieged by her rival, Stephen in 1142.

[4]

At this time, Oxford became a haven for wandering scholars from France and Italy. This was the beginning of the University of Oxford. There were already several learned religious foundations in the City: the College of Secular Canons of St. George beside the Castle, St. Frideswide Priory and Oseney Abbey (founded in 1129). Self-styled 'Masters of Oxford' gave lectures in increasing numbers, at first on the bible and law, later on a wider curriculum. By the beginning of the thirteenth century Oxford had developed its own *studium generale*, or University, with a seven-year programme of studies in the seven liberal arts (Grammar, Rhetoric, Logic, the Trivium; followed by the Quadrivium – Arithmetic, Geometry, Astronomy, Music). These were supplemented by courses in Philosophy and the three major professions (Theology, Law and Medicine). Before the middle of the century, the University had its own Chancellor, and became a self-governing institution.

Tension developed between this new University and the townsfolk – which has never completely disappeared, even to this day. Confrontations and riots occurred from time to time. The University, supported by both Church and Crown, usually prevailed. After the furious battle of St. Scholastica's day in 1355, a settlement was reached in which the City and University shared responsibility for the local government of Oxford. These provisions have largely disappeared in modern times.

In response to this ill-feeling between citizens and students, the earliest colleges began to appear in the fourteenth century to provide halls of residence, discipline and collegiate instruction for the young scholars – often as young as sixteen. University College, Balliol and Merton were the earliest of these, alongside Halls founded by the religious orders, Cistercians and Benedictines. Apart from the Church of St. Mary the Virgin on the High Street, the University owned little property at this time, functioning mainly in rented accommodation.

The college-model prospered and their numbers grew to fifteen in 1558. Meanwhile the Halls had reduced in number from fifty in 1450 to barely half a dozen a century later. There are no more than that today, but the University consists of almost forty colleges.

Meanwhile, Oxford had become an important market town. The walls, which still remain in places, were built in the thirteenth century, replacing earthen ramparts. Canute and Harold had held Councils there in the eleventh century. In the thirteenth century several Parliaments met at Oxford. But the town was in decline between then and the sixteenth century, overshadowed by the expanding and more-favoured University, which it served somewhat grudgingly.

The Renaissance and Reformation, which transformed Europe, made surprisingly little immediate difference to Oxford, although Erasmus, the leading scholar of the time, gave lectures there. Henry VIII created

[5]

a new bishopric, with its cathedral incorporated in his new college, Christ Church. Other colleges appear at this time, in some cases on the site and using the buildings of the religious Halls, closed at the time of the Dissolution of the Monasteries; and, of course, the new learning and new religion stimulated great academic debate and personal sacrifice. This was the time of the Oxford Martyrs, Cranmer, Latimer and Ridley, who were burned to death in Broad Street in 1555 and 1556, and are remembered by the Martyrs Memorial in St. Giles.

In the Civil War a century later, Oxford played a major role as the King's stronghold and headquarters. It finally surrendered to the besieging troops of Lord Halifax in 1646. As usual, Town and Gown took opposing sides: the University royalist, while the citizens secretly sympathised with the parliamentarians. Oliver Cromwell became Chancellor of the University in 1651, but it took many years before the resentments of the Civil War completely faded.

This was a time of rebuilding. The medieval University was enlarged, extended and reconstructed by the provision of new quadrangles in many of the Colleges and the addition of the Clarendon Building and the Sheldonian Theatre to provide a central focus for the University. In spite of this fervour of rebuilding, the University was in decline from the middle of the seventeenth century until the Victorian period some two hundred years later. Although Charles II held a parliament in Oxford in 1681 the University temporarily fell out of love with the Stuart monarchs – and then foolishly favoured the Jacobite cause against the Hanoverians in the eighteenth century. Oxford's bad habit of favouring the losing side in national politics has continued in modern times – most recently, with its opposition to Margaret Thatcher's government. The poet, Matthew Arnold, called Oxford 'the home of lost causes and forsaken beliefs'.

The City was gradually growing: the population numbered some 12,000 in 1801, but had increased to 27,000 by 1851. Soon after the dons were (at last) permitted to marry. They needed houses for their new wives and old mistresses (and children); it is said that Victorian North Oxford was created to provide them – though, in fact, much of this development was completed before 1877, when academic celibacy was officially abolished. Similarly, the establishment of the University Press in Walton Street led to the development of Jericho to provide artisan dwellings for its growing workforce. The railways (both GWR and LMS) arrived, making the Oxford Canal redundant within a few decades of its completion in 1790. By the end of the nineteenth century the population had increased to almost 50,000. The presence of a prospering University helped to create a desirable location for migrants from other parts of the UK, attracted by good schools, cultural amenities and an interesting social life. That is still true today, except that the immigrants come from all over the world.

Although John Wesley was a Fellow of Lincoln College, the religious reforms of Methodism largely passed Oxford by, while sweeping the rest of the country. Not so the Tractarian Movement, associated with the names of Keble, Pusey, and Newman. The Tractarians left a lasting legacy, still visible today both in the Church of England and the University of Oxford. The University was transformed in the nineteenth century by a series of major changes, often imposed from without by successive Royal Commissions. Written examinations were introduced, the range of studies extended, dissenters and women admitted, the academic profession and governance of the University reorganised. An expanding and progressive modern University emerged from its medieval predecessor. While much that was traditional remained, the substance was new. It is not too much to say that the University of Oxford received its re-foundation during the nineteenth century.

The twentieth century saw the City and University grow both in size and importance. By the mid-century the population had reached almost 100,000. Surrounding villages, like Cowley and Littlemore, were swallowed up in the urban expansion which followed the establishment of Morris Motors in east Oxford, transforming much of Oxford to the east of Magdalen Bridge into an industrial estate. Meanwhile, the University continued to grow and establish itself once more as one of the world's leading centres of learning.

Later in the century, the Oxford Polytechnic became the second University in Oxford (Oxford Brookes): it is a leading modern 'teaching first' institution complementing the ancient 'research first' University, which by the end of the century had completed the slow process of extending the curriculum to include modern subjects like Computing and Business Studies, and admitting women on a fully-equal basis to men. (They had not been permitted to take degrees before 1920.) Oxford is the focus for regional healthcare, with a range of first-class provision led by the relatively new JR Hospital in Headington. Excellence attracts excellence. These leading institutions are supported (in education) by a range of impressive colleges, language schools, private and state schools, and (in health) by a strong substructure of provision in private medicine and the National Health Service. Today, Oxford offers a first-rate infrastructure in all respects – save possibly the vexed issue of traffic management.

The City enjoys (near) full employment, even in periods of national recession. It is a rich City in a rich nation. It has a lively and diverse cultural life. But its remarkable history all too often seems to be a burden of inert tradition. Beneath a calm surface some unresolved tensions may be seen – between the worlds of learning, trade and industry (old manufacturing and new IT), for example, or between the three populations of residents, students, and tourists. Its most striking characteristic is an obsessive focus on the past, with a lack of serious interest in the future. While there is so much to be seen (and preserved), Oxford lacks vision for what it might be in years to come.

3. THE CHOICE OF THE SIGHTS

'Hope is a choice,' she said, 'like love'. And I,
Thinking of choices – blue or yellow tie?
Red wine or white? Radio 4 or 3?
Old-fashioned formal verse like this, or free
Modern (prosaic) poetry? – reflect
On whether we could possibly expect
People to *choose* their deepest feelings – hope,
Or love – and learn to escape the scripted soap-
Opera of so many lives.

                        I think
you should. Today, I'll wear a green tie, drink
a glass of rosé, try a CD, write
a poem with no line-initial caps. –
think noble thoughts, speak well, do what is right,
and choose to live in love and hope – perhaps?

CHOICE IS ARBITRARY AND INDIVIDUAL. We chose the sights illustrated here because we love them, and hope you will like them too. Of course, our readers, visitors and residents of Oxford, will enjoy making a list of sights which are unaccountably missing: Merton College, the Covered Market, South Park, Gloucester Green, the Divinity School, Lincoln College Chapel, or Minster Lovell (the seven missing sights?). Perhaps they could be included in a second edition of this book...

We are conscious that, unlike people, buildings seem to become more beautiful, the older they are. Who has ever seen an ugly Tudor building? It may be that beautiful buildings are well-constructed and more likely to survive the ravages of time, but we doubt it. A more likely explanation of the 'attractiveness of the ancient' is the very human habit of favouring what is familiar. We love what we know. Which is why almost all modern buildings are disliked to begin with. Time teaches us tolerance – and, in time, we learn to love what our forebears hated. Keble College is a prime example of this law of taste.

As a result, this selection of Oxford's sights is inevitably biased towards the past. Future generations will wonder why so little attention is given to the buildings of the twentieth century. *Le Tourisme Nouveau* requires the tourist to look only for buildings erected in their own lifetime – and seek to admire them: St. Catherine's College, the Said Business School, the Mosque or the Synagogue and the cooling towers of Didcot (soon to be demolished), for example. It is a difficult practice to master.

It is also true that our selection of sights was constrained by two requirements: that each sight would make a pleasing picture and inspire an interesting verse. In practice, the poem came first – and so the poet must bear the heavier responsibility for what was chosen, and what left out. So be it. We hope you also will enjoy the sights we love.

[9]

4. THE POEMS

One word or phrase, a cadence, starts
a poem. Like a hare, it bounds
across the page, checks, swerves and darts
forward again, intent on sounds
and sense, deceptive skills, the arts
of lying unobserved – still, warm
and safe, until at last it finds its proper form.

One verse, a metaphor, some wit:
simple to shape, hard to sustain.
Your oyster-poem requires grit,
a line that cuts across the grain,
before you feel you've finished it.
Poems transform, as they unfurl:
you must destroy the oyster to reveal the pearl.

One final verse makes all complete.
Endings are difficult. You seek
a resolution – apt and neat,
but not facile or pat. What's weak,
amend – and then, with a clean sheet,
relaunch your little craft, and get
the poem's form, its swelling sails, your pearl, well set.

TOPOGRAPHICAL POETRY – poems of place – is easy to write, but hard to make engaging or memorable. Descriptive verse is often felt to be inferior to the poetry of feeling – and so perhaps it is. These poems seek to address this difficulty by including, where possible, some human interest, challenging thought or critical judgment. The oil of description needs a dash of lemon juice to enliven it. The poems (like the paintings) are intended to encourage the reader and viewer to look more carefully at these sights and think more deeply about their significance.

The poet is a teacher and (like most teachers) rarely refrains from the practice of teaching anyone who will listen or read. Didactic poetry is quite unfashionable today – but we think it may be a fashion worth reviving. Incidentally, you may find that the poems take on new life when read aloud.

Most of the poems are written in formal verse: they have shape, stanzas, rhyme, lines of equal length (measured by syllables), and so on. They are *structured*, where free verse has no rules of structure – except that the lines never reach the right margin! See if you can spot the single example in this collection.

Some of the groups of seven poems have a common form. The first uses ten lines of ten syllables each; the second is a series of fourteen-line sonnets; the third includes stanzaic poems – with one exception written in blank verse. The fourth – the Seven Ages of Oxford – is different. Each poem seeks to imitate the verse style of the period described: for example, the poem about the University Museum echoes the style and form of Matthew Arnold's *The Scholar Gypsy*. There is less formal coherence and greater variety in the last three series, though the reader may notice poems which use a style or form appropriate to the subject (e.g. the Shelley Memorial, the Alfred Jewel or the Memorial Garden).

Oxford, of course, has been the home and nurse to many fine poets – and has inspired many others. There is a great tradition of Oxford verse – added to every year. I am glad to be a humble spear-carrier in that noble band.

[11]

5. THE PAINTINGS

'First, rule your neat horizon-line across
the page. Sketch cloud-capped mountain peaks above,
with trees below – their canopies should cut
the line – to give the picture depth. Then draw
a path with two converging lines from where
you stand to the horizon-line, which marks
the apex of the triangle. Complete
the picture, but remember that the line
of sight and the horizon share the same
apparent height. One-point perspective makes
true parallels appear to meet. The point
at the horizon's called *the vanishing point.*'

The vanishing point seems far off in our youth.
We climb those trees and scale the mountain-tops
to view distant horizons, stride along
that pathway in all weathers to compose
the pattern of our lives, forgetting that
our own horizon is determined by
the line of sight. For sedentary old age
brings the horizon closer; and the sick,
confined to bed in hospitals, can see
only a short distance ahead. Life's lines
converge at last in a one-point perspective.
People, like paths, must reach their vanishing point.

'WHEN I FIRST SET FOOT IN OXFORD in my teens I was awed and energised by it. Here was a place where you felt you needed a good book in your pocket for any idle moment – where the stones of the buildings themselves offered you encouragement to sit, read and think. Years later when I was asked if I might marry and consider living here, there wasn't a second of hesitation over moving from London. I love London, but Oxford has a scale for me that is more accessible – the perfect size to make you feel you might indeed get to know it well and yet be free to explore the wider spaces beyond. And that is to ignore its astonishing wealth of beauty and the real sense that anything is possible here. So many ideas have led to great changes in the world. Individuals count.

I can never tire of the pleasure of simply being here and looking at it, sharing it with excited visitors, frantic students cramming so much into a few short months they are given to live here, or permanent residents and businesses with the leisure to know it better. For me painting about its streets is a way to stop time and focus on detail. It seems ironical that someone incapable of drawing a straight line and with the patience of a flea (Is there a doctorate on the patience of fleas?) should choose to take such pleasure in attempting to capture its essence in paint. Yet, I feel privileged to be given the time to try to pay back a tribute to it visually, to try to catch the flickering rays of sun on old stone, water gently linking this town to others further up or downstream, the effect of detail on detail in all directions – some fanciful, some pious and all inspiring and life-enhancing.

My method has evolved from the need to be portable and for speed to attempt to capture time as well as place. First, a quick pencil sketch to compose the picture, followed by a swish of colours to convey the areas of sky, building and land and finally, perhaps my greatest pleasure, the ink sketch over this to draw in some of the detail, though not too much. Oxford has lifetimes-full to offer.' (K.S.)

[13]

6. THE WALKS

Along the dull canal – a flash of blue,
sudden, miraculous beneath gray skies,
enlightening our sodden walk – this
kingfisher flew.

The sight confirmed we live a lucky life.
We trudged along the towpath, pleased – ahead,
wearing her bright blue Pac-a-Mac, my wet
kingfisher wife.

Could such a day produce a further prize?
I glanced behind, and saw – not vivid birds –
but, shining from the west beyond the clouds,
kingfisher skies.

WE HAVE OFFERED six short walks around and through the centre of Oxford – and suggested the beginning and end of several longer ones in the series Seven Sights of Oxford. The others provide a convenient and interesting route, linking the seven sights in each section, starting and ending at Carfax, the crossroads at the centre of the City. Each walk is introduced and illustrated by a map and a commentary to ensure the visitor does not get lost. In all cases, the walks provide opportunities for rest and refreshment at one or other of Oxford's many restaurants, pubs or cafés. We recommend the visitor to explore the walks in the order they appear in the book – but it doesn't matter, if you reorder them. Several of them cover the same route in part: that is intentional – we wanted you to become familiar with our favourite streets and places in Oxford. These are (mostly) urban walks. No special footwear is required, but please be careful of the traffic when crossing roads. Cyclists can be a particular hazard.

7. AFTERWORD

Gone – the bright sun –
remain some rose-red streaks across the sky –
which fade – and, slowly, light – warmth – colour die –
the day is done.

A candle spent –
the bent black wick still smoulders – glows – and wanes –
thin smoke uncoils – vanishes – what remains? –
a fading scent.

When our lives cease –
expect no immortality – in hell
or heaven – nor lasting fame for things done well –
or ill – just peace.

WE HAVE GREATLY ENJOYED the experience of creating this book together. And now it is done. It was the outcome of a sequence of happy accidents. The first of these occurred some years ago when the artist and the poet – already friends, but not as yet artistic collaborators – drank a glass of champagne together in the Turrill Sculpture Garden behind the Summertown Library in South Parade (see p.128). We decided to paint a picture of, and write a poem about, this 'sculpture garden' and create a postcard from our joint work. We did – and sold them all.

Encouraged, we tried a more ambitious plan – to make a series of seven postcards, combining art and poetry, to celebrate the Seven Sights of Jericho, a precious older part of Oxford where one of us lives. These also sold well – though our retailers urged us to replace the pen-and-ink drawings with colour. We learned as we proceeded. We have discovered that we like each other's work, respect each other's views, and differ on some important questions. The artist is a faithful Jew, the poet a Christian atheist, for example!

The first two of the sequences of poems and paintings in this book were exhibited in Blackwell's Bookshop in 2010 and 2011. As a result our wise and generous publisher, James Ferguson, suggested that we should extend the series to create this volume. We wish to thank him, his designer, Andrew Esson – and Sebastian Ballard, who provided the maps – for all they have done to help us complete the project. We alone are responsible for any errors, intentional or unintentional, and apologise for the latter. We hope you enjoy the book, visit the sights, explore the walks and study our poems and paintings.

[17]

Port Meadow ⑦

St. Bernard's Rd

Bevington Rd

Old Pavilion ★ ⑥

University
Parks

River Cherwell

Walton Street

Keble Rd

✠ Fairisle Chapel

Oxford Canal

St. Giles

⑤

Trinity
College

Balliol
College

Broad Street

Beaumont St.

✠

④ ★

Radcliffe Square

Exeter
College

③

All Souls
College

Magdalen
College

Cornmarket

St. Mary's ✠

②

Magpie Lane

High Street

Magdalen
Bridge

★

Carfax

Merton College

St Aldgate's

✠

Deadman's Walk

Christ
Church

Merton Field
★

①

Christ Church
Meadow

River Thames

N

0   250
metres

© Mapman.co.uk (2013)

I. SEVEN SIGHTS OF OXFORD

WE HAVE CHOSEN THESE SEVEN SIGHTS (from many competitors) to provide an introduction to some of Oxford's most spectacular natural and architectural scenery.

The walk passes through the centre of the oldest part of the City, starting and ending in two of Oxford's finest areas of urban parkland, Christ Church Meadow to the south and Port Meadow to the north-west of the City.

Start from Carfax, the crossroads at the very centre of Oxford, and walk southwards down St. Aldate's, passing the Town Hall and Christ Church to your left. Enter CHRIST CHURCH MEADOW through the Memorial Gardens and explore this great open space. Students talk of a 'long Meadows' walk – turning right down the New Walk, then left along the river, which brings you back towards the City – or a 'short Meadows' walk – continuing straight on eastwards until you reach the river, turning left to follow Deadman's Walk below the old City Walls, now the southern boundary of Merton College.

Pass through a complicated iron gate, turning right to take the path between Merton and Corpus Christi Colleges leading to the cobbles of Merton Street. Cross over and walk up Magpie Lane to THE HIGH STREET, which you might explore in both directions – towards Carfax to your left, and Magdalen Bridge to the right.

Then, return to the junction with Magpie Lane, cross the High and walk through Catte Street to enter the remarkable RADCLIFFE SQUARE. Continue along Catte Street until you reach BROAD STREET. Turn left along this wide road, cluttered with parked cars, until you reach a crossroads – the Cornmarket to your left, Magdalen Street to the right. Turn right here and continue northwards into ST. GILES, taking the right fork past the War Memorial. Turn right almost at once along Keble Road.

At the end of Keble Road, cross Parks Road and enter THE UNIVERSITY PARKS. Here again, there is a choice between a 'long Parks' walk beside the river, a 'short Parks' walk around the cricket ground, or you could turn left immediately to walk northwards towards the gate at the north-west corner.

Pass through this, cross Parks Road again and the Banbury Road. Turn right – and then left at the next intersection to follow Bevington Road, St. Bernard's Road and Walton Well Road westwards over the canal and railway to reach PORT MEADOW. This huge expanse of grass and water offers a wide choice of shorter and longer walks along the river towards Wolvercote to the north.

Return the way you came along Walton Well Road, turning right into Walton Street, left at the end into Beaumont Street, then right along Magdalen Street and the Cornmarket to reach Carfax.

CHRIST CHURCH MEADOW

Between the Isis and the City wait
the Meadow, Merton Field and Deadman's Walk
(bordered by gardens you must pause to view)
beneath the spire of Christ Church and the towers
of Magdalen and Merton Colleges,
where many bells resound. As boats and hours
pass slow, the wise ones and the foolish talk
of tea and the eternal verities,
where one great river knits the flow of two,
while lonely souls and cattle ruminate.

The High Street

The noblest street in Europe is the High,
they say. Walk slowly down the sloping curve
from Carfax to the Plain. Admire the Church
(St. Mary's). Count the cloistered colleges.
Watch subfusc'd students scurry to the Schools
to demonstrate their learning and research
and prove they're new Duns Scotuses – not fools!
Linger on Magdalen Bridge to scan the sky,
the river and the City. Oxford is
a gem – to study, cherish and preserve.

RADCLIFFE SQUARE

Sir Thomas Bodley's library to the north
confronts the University's great Church
across the cobbled square, while to the west
and east lie Brasenose College and (research-
committed) All Souls; but the craziest
building's the Camera, behind its skirt
of grass and railings, trying to convert
squares into circles – store books on a curve!
Pause here, where line and shape work to preserve
the past in stone, before you venture forth.

BROAD STREET

Trinity's graceful College lies between
'the effortless superiority'
of Balliol, and Blackwell's store. Across
the busy street a range of buildings stand:
the Clarendon, Sheldonian (behind
the emperors), a quaint Museum, and
Exeter's northern face. Amid this scene
of solemn academic symmetry,
cohabiting with commerce, you may find
the rooftop figure and the inset Cross.

St. Giles

Pause in the centre of St. Giles where two
fine churches stand at either end, and where
across the busy street a noble pair
of Colleges confront the Roman Halls.
Ignore the traffic, contemplate the view
of twin Memorials to martyrdom –
of men who burned for a forgotten cause,
or sacrificed their lives in Europe's wars;
and listen to the restless leaves, the thrum
of distant gunfire and faint bugle calls.

THE UNIVERSITY PARKS

Between the Cherwell and big science blocks
besieging Keble's Fairisle Chapel find
the University's playground, the Parks,
where languid students laze in punts that pass
the pond where ducks come daily to be fed
towards the Rainbow Bridge – like little Arks –
and lively ones chase balls across the grass
around the old Pavilion painted white and red,
while dons discuss the latest paradox –
the nature of the cosmos, or the mind.

PORT MEADOW

Between the river and the railway lies
this great flood-plain, beneath still greater skies,
providing space for horses, ducks and herds
of cattle, dogs and children, men and birds,
to breathe and graze, to exercise and play
with soaring kites and sailing boats, away
from City streets and work, where green grass grows
from Wolvercote's frontier to Jericho's,
and water, air and clouds (or sunlight) please
the people and the animals at ease.

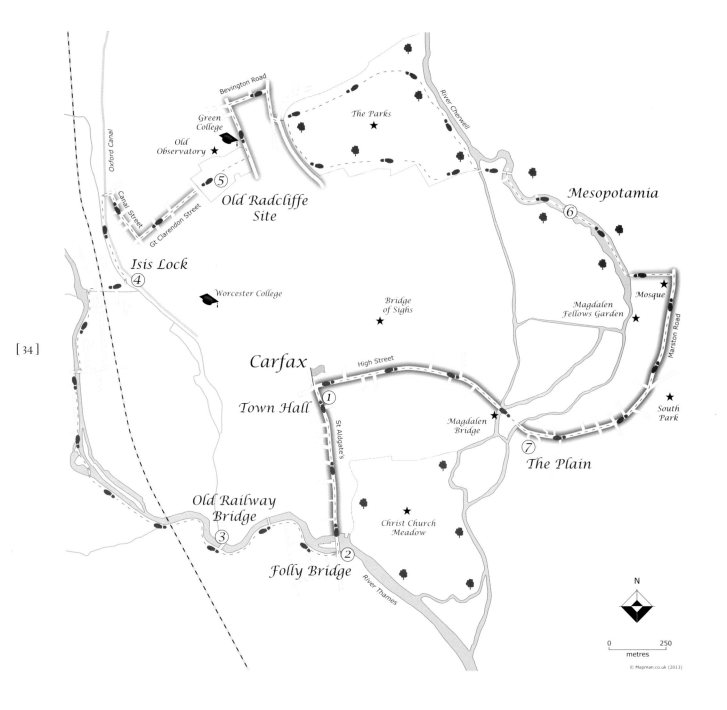

Bevington Road

Green College

Old Observatory ★

Oxford Canal

Canal Street

Gt Clarendon Street

⑤

Old Radcliffe Site

The Parks ★

River Cherwell

Mesopotamia

⑥

Isis Lock

④

Worcester College

Bridge of Sighs ★

Magdalen Fellows Garden ★

Mosque ★

Marston Road

Carfax

High Street

Town Hall

St Aldgate's

①

Magdalen Bridge ★

⑦

The Plain

South Park ★

Old Railway Bridge

③

②

Folly Bridge

River Thames

Christ Church Meadow ★

N

0 ——— 250
metres

© Mapman.co.uk (2013)

2. SEVEN SECRET SIGHTS

THE SEVEN SECRET SIGHTS are examples of some of Oxford's hidden beauties – rarely noticed by visitors and often overlooked even by residents.

The walk takes you in a circle around the centre of Oxford. Start from Carfax and walk southwards down St. Aldate's, where you will almost immediately find THE TOWN HALL on your left.

Continue along St. Aldate's to FOLLY BRIDGE, where you find the Thames towpath. Turn right – westwards, upstream – and follow the towpath to THE OLD RAILWAY BRIDGE. Continue along the towpath until you reach the Botley Road.

Cross it (carefully!), and then cross the bridge, to find the towpath continuing northwards. After you have crossed an arched footbridge, turn right, duck beneath the railway and follow the footpath to the ISIS LOCK.

This is the southern end of the Oxford Canal. Walk northwards along it and cross the first footbridge you find to enter Jericho. Follow Canal Street and Great Clarendon Street until you reach Walton Street. Cross it and enter THE OLD RADCLIFFE SITE, now in process of conversion to provide a new campus for the University of Oxford.

From the further side of the site join the Woodstock Road. Turn left, and then right into Bevington Road which takes you to the Banbury Road. Cross it and turn right, and then left, crossing Parks Road to enter The University Parks. Follow the path clockwise (or anti-clockwise, if you prefer!) to reach the south-east corner and MESOPOTAMIA, a hidden walk between two branches of the River Cherwell.

This path leads into King's Mill Lane and the Marston Road. Turn right past the Mosque and St. Clement's Church, and continue along St. Clement's Street to THE PLAIN. From there you can return across Magdalen Bridge and up The High to Carfax.

THE TOWN HALL

Oxford's magnificent Town Hall is worth
a visit. Climb the steps to find a space
where people meet and music's heard. This place
provides the City's civic centre. Birth
and death and marriage – joy and grief and mirth –
were registered here once; the Mayor's mace
is here; accounts of local history trace
an older Oxford buried in the earth.

So, ask to see the silver vault concealed
beneath this civic grandeur: narrow stairs
and locked doors hide an ancient Jewish house,
preserved unchanged for centuries. Here, prayers
were said, meals eaten, love exchanged, hurts healed –
before King Edward's dreadful 'Juden 'raus!'

FOLLY BRIDGE

Before the bridge was built, the cattle crossed
the river by a ford – the boundary
of Anglia and Wessex. Two or three
wooden bridges collapsed, burned down, were lost
in winter floods – and proved a heavy cost
to Oxford and its University.
Unusually, they managed to agree
that only fools would make a new impost
(or tax) to build another bridge. And so,
we call it Folly Bridge! That's one idea ...
Another is that dons think they possess
all wit and wisdom – folly starts right here
where Academia ends, the Thames! But no,
an architectural folly's a likelier guess.

THE OLD RAILWAY BRIDGE

With two rivers, a railway and canal
Oxford can boast – beside the towers and spires,
churches and pubs, it's famed for – several
fine bridges: Magdalen Bridge, Ball's Bridge – high-fliers
and humble arches – Hertford's Bridge of Sighs,
Folly Bridge and the bridges round the Ring
Road. Donnington and Swinford Bridges rise
above the Thames: close to the stream the swing-
bridge near the station lies disused. But my
especial favourite's the old railway arch
that once brought trains almost to the High
in Oxford's centre, derailed by the march
of time, now purposeless and idle, known
to few, except the ones who walk alone.

ISIS LOCK

The bridge at Isis Lock, where three ways meet,
invites reflection. North lies Banbury.
The lock allows canal-craft liberty
to segue westwards to the Thames, and greet
the punts and eights beyond the trains. Retreat
south to the City – nothing now to see
(except cars parked where once there used to be
a busy Port – replaced by rough concrete).

Look north along the towpath: Jericho's
derelict boatyard waits for restoration.
An old swing-bridge is hidden near the station,
while Worcester College to the east conceals
an earlier foundation. Search out those
secrets of Oxford. The lost past appeals.

THE OLD RADCLIFFE SITE

Here – for a time – survey this vacant space
where once a great Infirmary dispensed
care to the sick – and cures for some – now fenced,
guarded – a naked unregarded place.
Observe the old Observatory, and trace
time's footprint in the empty chapel and
redundant church at either end. You stand
where science, healing, love conjoined with grace.

All progress is deceptive: profit is
always partly offset by loss. The past
deserves respect – although it's wrong to fear
the future. So, look back – then turn at last
in hope, and trust the University's
fresh campus – new café – Green College, here.

MESOPOTAMIA

The land between two rivers fed the seeds
of our civilisation. Oxford's own
modest local Mesopotamia feeds,
protects and nurtures natural beauty – lone
swans, snowdrops by the river's edge, birdsong,
a weeping willow mirrored in the stream –
just weeds and woods and water. Stroll along
the path that links the Parks at one extreme
(with memories of Parsons Pleasure by
the weir) to Magdalen's Fellows Garden, where
flowers abound and notices deny
entry. Enjoy the views, the peace, the air.
Though this rare spot of *rus in urbe* may
seem safe, the City's never far away.

The Plain

Between the Mosque and Magdalen, South Park
and Christ Church Meadow, Cowley and the City,
you pass The Plain – a roundabout that's pretty
enough, but nothing special – and remark
the absence of any defining mark*
(some feature that might make The Plain less plain).
But listen with your heart, while I explain
what's present to your inner listening. Hark!

Forget the traffic, shops – where you can buy
cakes, party frocks, wine, oranges and lemons,
hard liquor and soft cheese for picnics by
the river's bank. Forget the racket – where
these five roads meet and merge – and try to hear
the silent sound of bells from old St. Clement's.

* *The displaced Carfax Conduit doesn't count.*

Inset map (Carfax, central Oxford):

N

To Blandon & Woodstock

St. Giles' Church

0 150
metres

St. Giles

War Memorial

To Hinksey

Nuffield College

Cornmarket

All Saints

St. Mary's

New Road

Carfax

High St.

To Cowley & Littlemore

Oxford Castle

St Aldate's

Christ Church

To Wantage

Main map:

N

0 3
km

Blenheim Palace ②

To Birmingham

To Birmingham

A44

A34

Charlton

Fencott

Murcott

Oddington

Noke

Otmoor ⑥

Beckley

Horton-cum-Studley

M40

Blandon

OXFORD

A40

To London

Harcourt Hill

①

Cowley

Le Manoir aux Quat' Saisons ⑤

A420

Jarn Mound

Littlemore

River Thames

③ Kelmscott Manor

A420

A34

Dorchester-on-Thames

To Reading & London

⑦ Abbey

The White Horse ④

Wantage

Wittenham Clumps

© Mapman.co.uk (2013)

3. SEVEN SIGHTS AROUND OXFORD

OXFORD IS SURROUNDED BY BEAUTY, as well as possessing so much of its own: a jewel in a worthy setting.

These seven sights are scattered around Oxford within a radius of about fifteen miles. Most visitors will probably wish to reach them by car or bus, although keen walkers could find them on foot. We have.

Four of them lie to the north-west (BLENHEIM PALACE), west (Kelmscott Manor, WESTWARDS FROM OXFORD), south-west (The White Horse, SOUTHWARDS FROM OXFORD) and east (Le Manoir aux Quat' Saisons, EASTWARDS FROM OXFORD).

Two (OTMOOR and DORCHESTER-ON-THAMES) lie a few miles away to the north-east and south-east.

That leaves one, APPROACHES TO OXFORD, which describes a variety of routes visitors may take to reach the City – accompanied by a painting of the River Thames.

The map shows the point of departure (Carfax), the beginning of the routes leading towards the four points of the compass and the termination points, together with the most important and interesting places mentioned in each of the seven poems.

APPROACHES TO OXFORD

If you have come to Oxford on the train
which pauses by the graveyard near the station,
look beyond Botley to where Wytham Woods
sleeps beneath skies which seem to promise rain.

Perhaps you came by car along a road
near Redbridge, Thornhill, Peartree or Seacourt,
where you can park and ride the bus to town –
and lend the charm of local names some thought.

But if you came by steamer up the Thames
past Iffley, Christ Church Meadow, Folly Bridge,
admire the ancient colleges you pass –
and wonder if they yet teach wisdom's gems.

Some come on foot, and others cycle here
by the canal or over Cumnor Hill
where Clough and Arnold walked, and found their tree –
and thought the Scholar-Gypsy lingered still.

City of walls and books, tall towers, deep
ideas, where people come to get degrees
and postcards, drink a cup of tea or learn:
a patchwork formed of words and stones and trees –

and those who seek the truth, like Scotus once,
poor Cranmer, Wesley, Keble, who all meant
it when they said, 'God is my light', before
we understood the true Enlightenment.

BLENHEIM PALACE

If you leave Oxford by the Northgate, note
the War Memorial near St. Giles's Church,
the two Parades where Cromwell and the King's
armies confronted one another; search

for hidden signs of warfare in a City
apparently so peaceful: Town and Gown
rioting in the streets, the Castle raised
to seal the triumph of the Norman Crown.

Then travel further northwards towards Woodstock
and visit Bladon – honour Churchill's grave.
Remember him, who offered blood, toil, sweat
and tears, one chosen by the King to save

his nation, which he did. Give thanks for that.
Then cross the road to view the majesty
of Blenheim Palace, where the Duke of Marlborough
enjoyed the nation's gratitude, when he

won famous battles for another King.
Oxford is soaked in history; it stains
the stones and haunts the memory.
The past is never lost. Some trace remains.

WESTWARDS FROM OXFORD

If you leave Oxford by the Westgate past
Lord Nuffield's College, setting out towards
the other William Morris's grand house
at Kelmscott (where he taught: 'keep nothing but
what's beautiful and useful') – you may come
to know a City, not devoted only
to study, science, culture, leisure and
the past, but one also concerned with work,
the dignity of labour. Duck beneath
the railway, cross the river, find the path
to Hinksey Ruskin made to teach his students
to practise making things, not just admire
them (though his road's not worthy of an A!),
then climb up Harcourt Hill to reach the track
which leads you to a strange and man-made pile –
Jarn Mound – constructed by the unemployed
between the Wars. Their work was paid for by
Sir Arthur Evans, who revealed the lost
Minoan civilisation in Crete –
and made this Mound to help the climbers view
the transient civilisation of Oxford.

SOUTHWARDS FROM OXFORD

If you leave Oxford by the Southgate – long
forgotten – passing Christ Church, once the college
named for Cardinal Wolsey, where the students
seek fame and fortune (through learning and knowledge),

reflect upon the transience of things.
Fortune is fickle; fame must slowly fade;
wealth, when secured, seems worth a good deal less;
quicksilver power's, once grasped, at once mislaid.

The Vanity of Human Wishes. Look
across St. Aldate's to the college where
the author (Dr. Johnson) studied once –
poor, unpreferred, and prone to black despair.

All human life is meaningless at last.
Walk on to Wantage, birthplace of a king,
Alfred the Great, remembered (if at all)
today, not for his greatness, but a thing

both trivial and (probably) untrue:
burnt cakes. At least he's not forgotten (yet)
unlike whoever hoped to be remembered
by the White Horse. There's no name to forget.

EASTWARDS FROM OXFORD

If you leave Oxford by the Eastgate, down
the High, you pass All Saints, St. Mary's and
the site of old St. Clement's on the Plain –
with college chapels close on either hand.

Go on to Cowley; ponder Newman's last
Anglican sermon preached at Littlemore;
Remember the grave Cowley Fathers; mark
the many littered churchyards here, before

you pass by Temple Cowley, and at length
reach open country. Oxford's a museum
of moribund religion: church bells ring
unheeded, choristers intone *Te Deum*

to empty pews, priests preach eternal life
and sacrificial love to faithless ears.
But, look again! The new religion's come –
one disappears, another god appears!

We worship food today – on every side
see delis, cafes, pubs and restaurants,
where you can buy exotic meals or plain
old English dishes: tapas – tea and scones.

Forget the road to Canterbury, Rome,
Jerusalem: you seek Le Manoir aux
Quat' Saisons, the cathedral of the new
devotion – here's the shrine where foodies go.

New temples rise, replacing those that fall.
Enjoy your meal – be mindful, as you munch
your *amuse bouche,* that nothing lasts
for ever, no, not life, nor love – nor lunch.

OTMOOR

Otmoor's a nothing place – or so one thinks,
when first appears this empty, marshy waste,
low-lying in a shallow bowl of land –
a rifle range, some birds – but make no haste

to judge this strange site, where a Roman road
once crossed, and where the ghost of an unmade
motorway lingers still, a trackless waste
hospitable to boots – and tractors: shade-

less, silent, lonely, with the Seven Towns
of Otmoor ranged around it: Beckley, Noke,
Oddington, Charlton, Fencott, Murcott and
Horton-cum-Studley. *There* find food and folk

and friendship; *here* one may yet see a trace
of Alice's chessboard, or hear the faint
echo of riots incited by the forced
Enclosure Act of 1815. Paint,

nor words, does justice to this special spot
reserved for nature – birds and butterflies –
half-flooded by the River Ray, where starlings
numberless flock to roost whilst daylight dies.

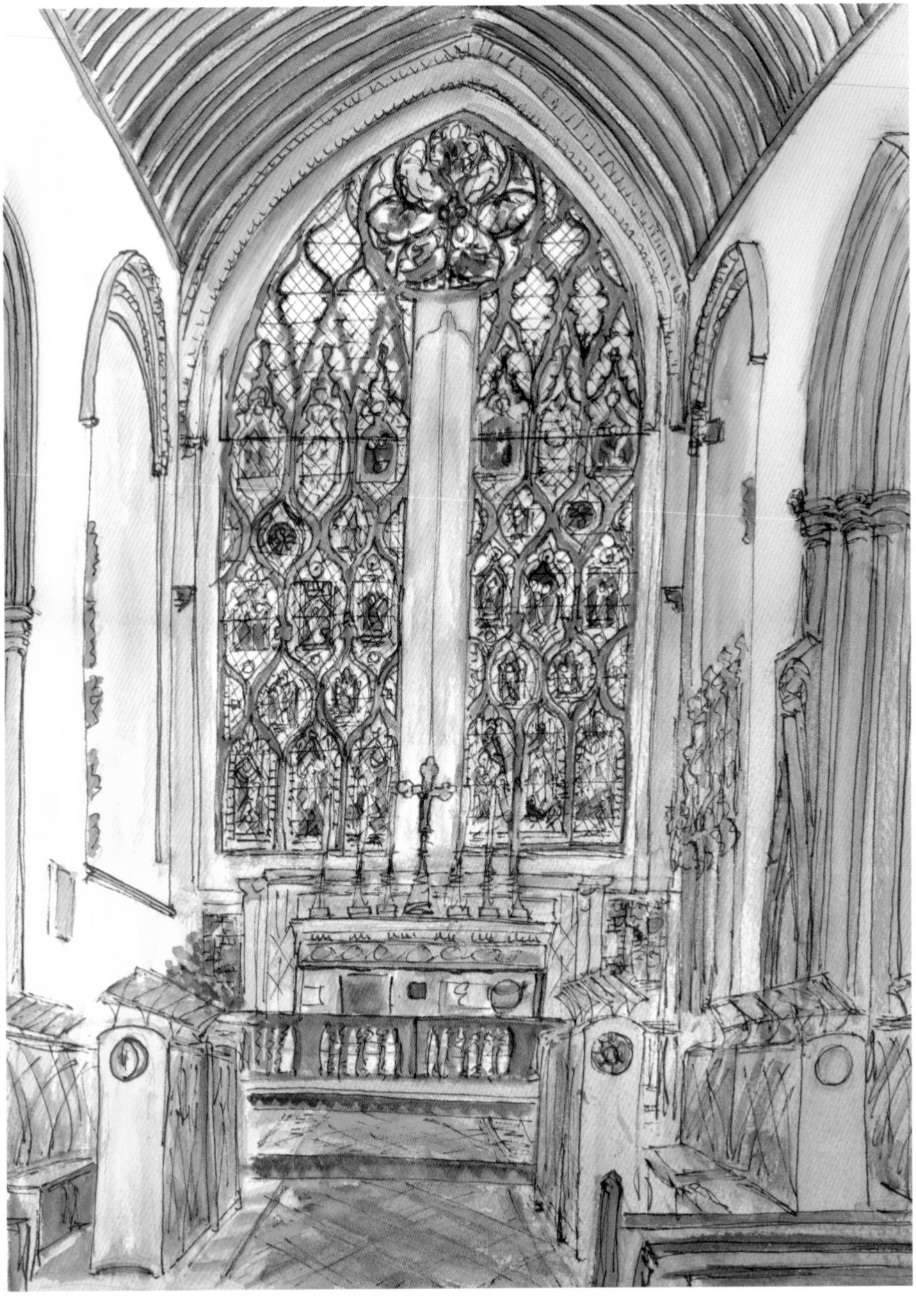

DORCHESTER-ON-THAMES

This is a something place: the river's curve
nudges the flood-plain, while the dyke
protects the town from water – where the tower
of Dorchester's great Abbey rises boldly like

a pillar pointing us towards the skies.
Across the Thames, walkers climb a low mound,
Wittenham Clumps, to seek a vantage point
to view the works of men and nature all around.

The plain, the river and the hills predate
our human history. Nature began
to shape the land and form its features: each
in turn received its own distinctive name from man.

Though *Thames* is Celtic – like most river names,
the town is an old Roman army camp –
a Saxon bishopric – the Abbey Norman, but
the later centuries have also left their stamp.

Look at the Jesse Window and the font:
the furnishings and glass are very fine.
Then stroll through Dorchester to find the inns,
where travellers can stay and you may rest and dine.

Men made this place – and it survives unspoilt
by modern blocks, at least for a few brief
years – although you may find convenient
the new PC, providing tourists with relief.

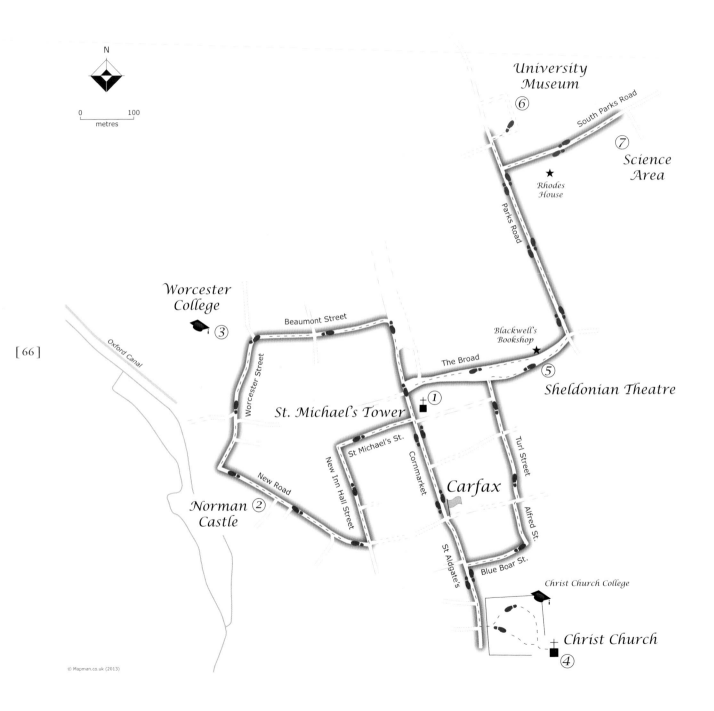

N

100
metres

Oxford Canal

Worcester
College ③

Beaumont Street

Worcester Street

St. Michael's Tower

New Road

New Inn Hall Street

St Michael's St.

Cornmarket

Norman
Castle ②

① +

The Broad

Blackwell's
Bookshop

Sheldonian Theatre

⑤

Turl Street

Carfax

Alfred St.

St Aldgate's

Blue Boar St.

Christ Church College

Christ Church
④ +

University
Museum
⑥

South Parks Road

⑦ Science
Area

Parks Road

Rhodes
House

© Mapman.co.uk (2013)

4. SEVEN AGES OF OXFORD

OXFORD'S HISTORY (briefly summarised in the Introduction) stretches back over some 1200 years to the time of King Alfred – and (no doubt) forwards over many more to create further ages for this remarkable City. We present it here as a unfinished story in seven illustrated chapters.

The walk takes you through some of the most interesting – and memorable – parts of the City, while following a historical pathway through seven ages of Oxford.

Start at Carfax and walk northwards along the Cornmarket. As you approach the traffic lights, observe St. Michael's Church on the right-hand side with its SAXON TOWER (c. 1000).

Cross the road and walk down St. Michael's Street. Turn left into New Inn Hall Street, and then right at Bonn Square into Queen Street and New Road. The eleventh-century NORMAN CASTLE is on the left, surrounded by modern restaurants.

Continue down New Road and turn left into Worcester Street. Follow this road northwards, crossing Hythe Bridge Street at the lights, until you reach the intersection with Beaumont Street. WORCESTER COLLEGE (once Gloucester Hall, founded in the later thirteenth century) is on the left.

Now walk up Beaumont Street, turning right into Magdalen Street and continue southwards along the Cornmarket, past Carfax, and down St. Aldate's, to find CHRIST CHURCH (1532; refounded in 1546) on the left-hand side.

Retrace your steps a short distance towards Carfax, turning into Blue Boar Street just before the Town Hall. Follow this narrow lane and then turn left at the end into Alfred Street. Cross the High Street and walk through Turl Street to the Broad. Here you should turn right to find the SHELDONIAN THEATRE (later seventeenth century), opposite Blackwell's Bookshop.

Now continue to the eastern end of Broad Street. Turn left into Parks Road and walk northwards to find the UNIVERSITY MUSEUM (1855) on the right, opposite Keble College.

Finally, retrace your steps a short distance and turn left into South Parks Road. This is the University of Oxford's SCIENCE AREA (nineteenth-twenty-first centuries).

Return to Carfax along Parks Road, the Broad Street and the Cornmarket.

Saxon Oxford: St. Michael's Tower

Oxford enters the annals of history
in Saxon times as a trading centre,
where four roads meet by a ford for cattle.
Walk from Carfax along the Cornmarket
to see St. Michael's, besieged by commerce,
the City Church with its Saxon tower,
the oldest building in Oxford today.
A Saxon poet impressed by ruins,
Roman remains and the marvels of Stonehenge,
wrote of ancient structures established by giants.
But the Saxon masons also mastered construction
before the end of the first Millennium.
Forget the styles and stonework that followed,
medieval or modern, that Oxford abounds in –
admire for a moment St. Michael's tower.

NORMAN OXFORD: THE CASTLE

After the Conquest, William made
certain his power would be displayed
to the defeated Saxon race
by building castles. Every place
of note was fortified. The Tower
of London is new Norman power
made visible. In Oxford, he
told Robert D'Oyly, 'Build for me
a modern castle on a mound.'
The Norman Governor soon found
a western site beyond the Gate.
His workmen toiled to fabricate
a wooden structure – stone came later
to make the Castle even greater.
It proved a prison fit for Queen
Matilda: prison it has been
for centuries, until today –
when visitors like you can stay –
transformed into a fine hotel
whose guests sleep in their narrow cell.

Oxford University: the first colleges

Wandering scholars were the first of many wise professors
who came from Paris long ago and stayed to teach in Oxford.
In time, these doctors formed a new *studium generale*,
an English University, like Paris or Bologna.
The University acquired a Chancellor, and courses
of studies in the Liberal Arts, Philosophy, professions –
Theology, Law, Medicine – with halls of residence for
the students, drawn from far and wide to qualify as Masters.
Dan Chaucer's Clerk was one of these: he loved a book at bedtime.
The halls and colleges began to grow in number, founded
`by wealthy men and women, John de Balliol and his widow,
Walter de Merton, others. University's the oldest
real college, but the halls were more numerous at the outset,
established and supported by the great religious houses,
Dominicans and Carmelites, Franciscans, Benedictines –
whose Gloucester College still survives (renamed as Worcester College,
after the Reformation swept away monasticism).
You still can see how colleges and halls began as humble
cottages owned by Masters who were licensed to admit some
students and teach them: the Front Quad retains a row of dwellings
facing the classical north range, a relic of old Oxford.

REFORMATION OXFORD: THE KING'S COLLEGE

1. The Cardinal's Account

Mine first – and named by me the Cardinal's
College – this Christ Church is my legacy.
The Hall is mine – not Hogwarts'! You can see
My statue over the Great Gate, the bell's
Great Tom, which summons scholars home, and tells
Each night the local curfew faithfully.
The Great Quadrangle was designed by me –
With cloisters, still unbuilt. The pride, that swells

Before the fall, here flaunts itself. I fell.
I'd failed to make reforms in church affairs;
Port and preferments I preferred to prayers;
My Star Chamber men feared, as men fear Hell;
I'd failed to help the King exchange his wife.
I lost my place, my college and my life.

2. The King's Answer

The King of England answers to no man –
Not Prelate, Pope, nor foreign Prince, no power
On earth. We govern absolutely. Can
I not commit whom I will to the Tower?
This college is my College, re-endowed
By me, who made a new Cathedral here
To preach and teach my new religion. Loud
The organ plays, choir chants, throughout the year
To celebrate a Nation unified,
A Church reformed, a Monarchy made great,
A College re-established to provide
Good learning to new leaders of our State.
    So long as England lasts, and Kings shall be,
    So long stands this – a monument for me!

CLASSICAL OXFORD: THE SHELDONIAN THEATRE

All human things are subject to decay;
And when style changes, Oxford must obey.
Its medieval architecture was
Untidy – and, in time, unloved – because
The neo-classic age liked harmony,
Neat regularity and symmetry.
Saint Mary's Church no longer satisfied
The university's need to provide
A place for academic festivals
And ceremonies – often breeding brawls
And riots, unbecoming in a church.
So Gilbert Seldon, after a long search
For the best living architect, chose Wren,
Professor of Astronomy, who – when
Seldon agreed to pay the costs – designed
The Theatre that bears his name. You'll find
Its shape is half a circle, half a square.
The painter's art and architecture share
The credit for the ceiling, for its time
A masterpiece, as skilful as sublime.

VICTORIAN OXFORD: THE UNIVERSITY MUSEUM

The Scholar Gypsy waited for the spark
From Heaven, but Matthew Arnold only heard
The melancholy, long, withdrawing roar
Of the great Sea of Faith that used to gird
Our human shores. In here, the dinosaur
Reminds us that nothing survives death's dark
Extinction: no, not creeds nor creatures. Men
And monkeys, species, cities, cultures, cults,
Artists and poets die. All life results
In death. Nothing, and no one, lives again.

Imagine, if you will, the great debate
Between the Bishop and the Scientist
On evolution, Darwin's strange idea,
Held here. Today's Creationist
Is an endangered species, now it may appear
There is no God who intervenes. We wait
In vain for any spark from heaven. This
Museum's dodo and its dinosaur
Tell visitors they also must explore,
One day, extinction in death's deep abyss.

Modern Oxford: the Science Area

Modern Oxford's a disappointment.
Where's the iconic building
that represents the age?
The multi-storey car park? – or the Mosque? –
 Brookes University? – or the Business School
beside the fast-decaying station? –
the Old Radcliffe site in transformation
to provide another new campus? –
or the ever-growing JR Hospital
up on the hill?

The Clarendon Centre in the Cornmarket,
and the Westgate development
that swept away the charms
of old St. Ebbe's,
the mobile kebab vendors
and the ice-cream vans,
feeding our insatiable appetites,
demonstrate that commerce
conquers everything:
Oxford is still a trading City first.

But walk down South Parks Road –
study the disorganised
development of science
(beside redundant Rhodes House,
relic of a lost empire).
Here is the new enlightenment,
more precious than money,
kinder than campaigners,
wiser than religions.
Our best hope of truth.

Binsey
Church

⑦

Perch
Inn

River Thames

Port
Meadow

Keble Chapel

⑤

Keble College

Ashmolean Museum

Walton Street

Parks Road

Bodleian Library

New College Chapel

⑥

St.Giles

④

③

Shelley Memorial

Oxford Canal

Cornmarket

B

②

Carfax

High St.

The Upper
Reaches

Christ
Church
Meadow

Folly Bridge

River Thames

Iffley Road

B

Church Way

Iffley Turn

N

0   500
metres

Iffley Lock

①

St. Mary's

© Mapman.co.uk (2013)

5. SEVEN TREASURES OF OXFORD

We have chosen seven of our favourite places in the City to represent 'treasures of Oxford'. We could have found many more.

The walk begins at St. Mary's Church in Iffley. Take a bus from Queen Street or the Queen's Lane stop in the High Street to Iffley Turn. Follow Church Way to find this well-preserved Norman Church.

Return to Oxford via Iffley Lock and the towpath beside the Thames. Cross Folly Bridge and enter Christ Church Meadow through the gate behind The Upper Reaches. Walk along the river round the Meadow to the gate to Rose Lane, which leads to the High Street. Turn left and continue up the High until you come to the entrance to University College on the left-hand side. Here is the Shelley Memorial.

Cross the High Street, turn right, and then left into Queen's Lane, leading to New College Lane, where you find an entrance giving access to New College Chapel (in visiting hours). The main entrance to the College is in Holywell Street.

[83]

Continue along New College Lane beneath the Bridge of Sighs and cross Catte Street to find the Bodleian Library. Walk northwards along Catte Street and cross the end of Broad Street to reach Parks Road. Follow this tree-lined avenue until you find Keble College, built of multi-coloured brick, on the left. Keble College Chapel is your objective.

Now retrace your steps a short distance along Parks Road and turn right into Museum Road, leading to the Lamb and Flag passage and St. Giles. Turn left, and then right into Beaumont Street, where you will find the Ashmolean Museum on the right-hand side. Here is the Alfred Jewel.

Finally, make your way down Beaumont Street, turn right into Walton Street, and walk to the end (where it becomes Kingston Road). Then turn left down Walton Well Road and cross the canal and railway to enter Port Meadow. Continue westwards across the Meadow to find a gate leading to a low bridge spanning a subsidiary branch of the river. Cross it and turn right onto the towpath. This takes you across an attractive arched bridge to the further side of the river. Turn right (you have no choice!) and continue northwards until you meet a path branching left across a muddy field shortly before you reach the Perch Inn. This path leads to a minor road: follow it (to the right) through Binsey village until it peters out at Binsey Church.

Return to Carfax the way you came – along the towpath, across Port Meadow, via Walton Well Road, Walton Street, Beaumont Street, Magdalen Street and the Cornmarket.

A Carol for St. Mary's, Iffley

After the shepherds and the kings
Were gone – with that angelic band –
Silence returned, and normal things:
The parents troubled, watchful – and
   The little child
Asleep, the animals awake.
The stable smelt. And it was cold.
What sense could any of them make
Of kings and angels, star and gold?
   But Jesus smiled.

'This child needs changing,' Joseph said.
'It's your turn, dear,' said Mary, 'I've
Just done my bit. I clothed and fed
Our first-born. I brought forth alive
   This darling child.'

Like us, they argued – and like us
They spoke what they would soon regret.
As nothing can placate our fuss,
So nothing could resolve their fret –
   Till Jesus smiled.

Now centuries have come and gone,
The story's spread from land to land,
Since Matthew, Mark and Luke and John
First told us of those parents and
   That precious child.
Remember Him, remember them –
The promise of that distant birth:
Goodwill and peace in Bethlehem,
Peace and goodwill in all the earth,
   When Jesus smiled.

SHELLEY'S MEMORIAL

'Life, like a dome of many-coloured glass,
Stains the bright radiance of eternity.' (*Adonais*)

His life was brief; he dazzled, and is dead.
He lies as if asleep, unclothed and pale,
drowned in a storm off Lerici, his bed
the sun-warmed sand, his shroud the sea-stained sail
ripped from the boat wrecked in that sudden gale
that stole his life and stopped the flow of verse
that once inspired the nation's youth to scale
the frowning heights of tyranny, and curse
injustice. Sans his words, the world would be the worse.

For one short year this College was his home,
his nurse, his mentor: it rejected him.
But now his image rests within this dome –

this irreligious man lit by a dim
religious light, where art conceals the grim
reality of death, where family
piety – and remorseful College – trim
the truth, and prompt the visitor to see
a comfortable scene, less fact than fantasy.

Forget this picture: read his poems now:
the Odes or *Ozymandias*, his plays –
The Cenci is the best – his prose. Learn how
this strange anarchic poet learned to daze
and dazzle readers. Study *Adonais,*
the lyrics or the longer poems. Mind
you do not fail to turn your curious gaze
on *A Defence of Poetry*, and find
this unacknowledged legislator of mankind.

New College Chapel

The Chapel, like the College, like the City,
is best seen from inside: a precious store
of treasure – architecture, decoration,
choir-stalls and windows, reredos ... and more.

Look at the sunlight staining the pale stonework;
listen to music – choir and organ – or
feel those five hundred years' worth of tradition
contained within this building ... and there's more.

El Greco's painting of St. James (self-portrait?)
and Epstein's Lazarus – who must deplore
his life's renewal with the loss of heaven.
That isn't all. The Chapel holds still more.

Study the War Memorial for the members
of New College now on that further shore
and in a greater light – or not – and ponder
the meaning of such sacrifice. There's more.

You search the transept for another, smaller,
simple memorial, close to the door,
for those who fought us once. Such perfect manners,
true courtesy! That's all. There's nothing more.

This modest second First World War Memorial's
the finest thing in Oxford. Stand in awe
to read the names of those four German scholars
and soldiers, honoured here for evermore.

The Bodleian Library

I wish I'd been there when the first
  humans invented language. Speech
connects: they talked, they taught, conversed
  and questioned, each with each.

I wish I'd been there when the wise
  Egyptians learned to write –
record their thoughts; retrieve, revise
  their words – bring sounds to sight,

inaugurating history
  five thousand years ago.
Writing replaces memory;
  books store what people know.

This is the finest book-store on
  the earth – four hundred years
to make; it will, in less, be gone.
  All treasure disappears

in time. New ages generate
  new modes of info-tech:
the Web will soon invalidate
  the book, computers check

the flow of print. Libraries are
  redundant now. Regret
is futile: as the motor car
  replaced the horse, the Net

makes books antiques, like chamber pots
  and Pyramids. What's here
is a museum filled with lots
  of old books. Shed a tear:

I almost wish I'd not been born
  to see the Internet
inaugurate another dawn –
  the age of books' sunset.

A Hymn for Keble Chapel

'Learn to love, and leave all other.'
(William Langland)

Teach us to love, true God of love,
This rich creation, creatures rare –
Earth, apple, Adam, serpent, Eve –
Secure in their Creator's care.

Teach us to love our families –
Father and daughter, mother, son –
Help us love them as they love us,
To bear and to forbear at home.

Teach us to love our enemies,
Help us to serve those whom we hate,
To cherish those who challenge us,
And see in sin the seeds of grace.

Teach us to love those we adore –
The soul-in-flesh to recognise –
Teach us the care at passion's core –
To make, and take, love's sacrifice.

Teach us to love ourselves at last,
That others we may love as well,
And, knowing value in this dust,
We love our neighbours as ourself.

Teach us to love the God of love,
Veiled, but ubiquitous as air,
Stronger than death, impulse of life,
Heart of creation everywhere.

Teach us to love, true God of love,
This rich creation, creatures rare –
Earth, apple, Adam, serpent, Eve –
Secure in their Creator's care.

THE ALFRED JEWEL

'Þaes ofereode, Þisses swa mæg' (*Deor*)

'Alfred had me made.' The Anglo-Saxon king
(who burned the cakes and beat the Danes)
the only king or queen called 'great'
in English history, ordered this jewel
from his craftsmen to accompany a book,
his *Pastoral Care*, as a pointer-cum-bookmark.
  Those days are gone; these too will pass.

Or did he? Scholars doubt that a king
as great as Alfred would ever allow
his name to appear naked, untitled,
as here – although there are some coins
minted at Oxford where Alfred's name
also appears without any title.
  Those days are gone; these too will pass.

One possible answer is found in the Preface to the book,
where Alfred addresses each of his bishops
by name and status, starting with himself:
'King Alfred greets …' Some argue that the Jewel's
text is a postscript to the Preface, obviating
a second title, since the two were to be inseparable.
  Those days are gone; these too will pass.

But I prefer by far the idea
that the missing pointer (mark the socket)
was made of precious metal and inscribed
with the missing title – and may even turn up one day
to complete the message, and make a metrical verse-line.
'Alfred had me made – the English nation's king.'
  Those days are gone; these too will pass.

Where should we search? The Somerset marshes
near Athelney are where the Alfred Jewel was discovered –
close to the monastery the monarch had founded.
Its Abbot was called John, a German scholar, one of the
team of Latinists who had translated the book
Alfred wished to send to every see in his kingdom.
Those days are gone; these too will pass.

The Alfred Jewel's unanswered questions
tease careful scholars and casual visitors,
perplex the poet and surprise historians:
who is the figure with flowers in his hands?
Alfred himself? or perhaps Saint Cuthbert?
or God in his glory above a glassy sea?
  Those days are gone; these too will pass.

The past is a storehouse of precious things:
curious fragments and confusing questions,
stories and objects, strangeness and sameness.
Museums remind us of the mysteries of time:
everything changes, everyone dies.
Our age will vanish, as Alfred's has done.
  Those days are gone; these too will pass.

BINSEY CHURCH

Here is a sacred superstitious spot,
beloved of families who like to walk –
before the costly gifts and festive dish,
the Christmas commerce round the wassail pot,
amidst the idle chat and trivial talk –
   to mouth a prayer, or make a wish.

Start from the Walton Well in Jericho;
cross the canal and railway – there's a train!
Continue westward towards Medley Weir;
north over Misprint Bridge (you missed it?). Go
along the towpath, muddy track and lane:
   a church beside a well is here.

St. Frideswide's Well – St. Margaret's Church:
two saints,
each known from story more than history.
One dwelt near Oxford, one in Antioch:
two virgins voicing similar complaints
against male lust, which mocks the chastity
   of any figure in a frock.

Frideswide was chased by Lanfranc, but her prayer –
for praying then was valid – struck him blind.
St. Mary's miracle made him repent.
Frideswide invoked St. Margaret to repair
the harm; well-water cured him; so, you find
   today this double monument.

Walk on to Godstow by the Thames, and see
the ruins of a nunnery, destroyed
by Henry: royal power made manifest.
(He knew what's real and what's imaginary!)
Return to Oxford, once you have enjoyed
   refreshment at The Trout, and rest.

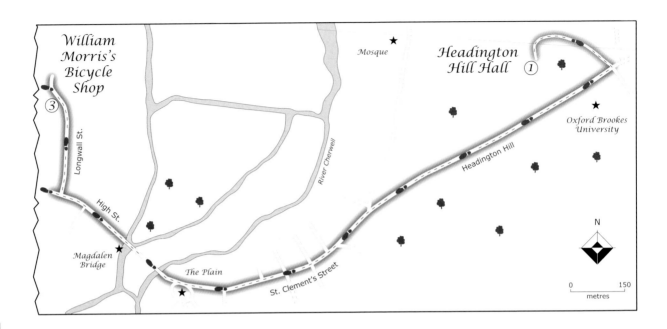

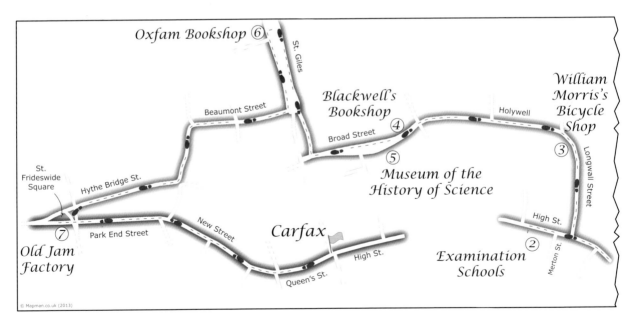

6. SEVEN PRODUCTS OF OXFORD

WE HAVE CHOSEN SEVEN products for which Oxford is – or has been – famous: beer, books, charity, learning, marmalade, motor-cars and technology. The list is, of course, not exhaustive.

The walk starts at HEADINGTON HILL HALL. Take a bus from Queen's Lane in the High Street to Brookes University. The Hall is the administrative centre of the University, located in parkland near the top of the hill on the left-hand side.

Walk back to Oxford down Headington Hill, along St. Clement's Street, passing The Plain and crossing Magdalen Bridge. Continue into the High Street where, after passing the entrance to Merton Street on the left-hand side, you come to THE EXAMINATION SCHOOLS.

Now retrace your steps to the traffic lights. Cross the High Street and walk up Longwall Street to find WILLIAM MORRIS'S BICYCLE SHOP on your left.

Continue along Longwall Street. Turn left into Holywell, which leads you to Broad Street. Here you will find BLACKWELL'S BOOKSHOP on the right-hand side and (almost opposite, just beyond the Sheldonian Theatre) the Museum of the History of Science, where you can study the development of science and TECHNOLOGY.

Continue along Broad Street to turn right into Magdalen Street and St. Giles. Continue until you find the Oxfam Bookshop on the left-hand side, providing an opportunity for CHARITY.

Return southwards along St. Giles and turn right into Beaumont Street, then left at the end into Worcester Street, which bends to the right to become Hythe Bridge Street. Follow this route towards the railway station and St. Frideswide's Square, where you will find the old JAM FACTORY on the left. Return to Carfax from the south-east corner of the Square along Park End Street, New Road and Queen Street.

HEADINGTON HILL HALL

Headquarters of Brookes great University today,
      a centre of learning;
this building is where Robert Maxwell's Pergamon Press
      produced his books once;
earlier still, it was the home of the Morrell family,
      the local brewers.

Beer, books and brains are odd bedfellows,
      a strange conjunction.
The more I drink, the less I write – or know.
      Beer makes men brainless.
To hold the balance, Oxford gave us John Wesley,
      who preached abstinence.

Writing, research and learning require a methodology,
      not methomania.
Where are the Methodists to keep us straight?
      Their voices are fading.
But down the hill, across the Marston Road,
      the Mosque reminds us

of the Five Practices of Islam, which provide a method.
      or rule to live by:
study and fasting, alms-giving, prayer and pilgrimage –
      a cogent doctrine
for us all. Walk and read, reflect, donate –
      and drink some water.

[102]

THE EXAMINATIONS SCHOOLS

'What we learn, we learn by doing.' (Aristotle)

    (A child, engrossed, is climbing steps
    and counting: 'One-and-two-and-three'.)

Here the Masters and the Doctors give instruction,
    and students learn.
Here the Dons examine candidates, each hoping
    to qualify –
Bachelors of Arts, Philosophy or Science –
    equipped to earn
decent salaries in graduate employment,
    and reach the sky!

Here's the standard form of modern education:
    teach and assess –
commonplace in universities and schoolrooms.
    So, does it work?
Well enough – provided knowledge matters more
    than skill does, I guess.
But it's *competence* one needs: *doing* the business.
    (*Knowing*'s a perk!)

    ('... and-four-and-five ...' She pauses, poised
    on one small foot, and looks at me.)

Medieval Oxford's pedagogy differed
    in several ways:
commensality required that students keep terms
    and eat together –
periods of residence, a common table,
    prayers and praise.
This regime transmitted skill and culture well – the
    question's whether

this old system of apprenticeship (we call it
    'sitting by Nellie')
can do more than pass the baton of tradition
    and replicate
skills and insights gained already. Though a student
    learns them well, he
lacks the quality of independence making
    true scholars great.

    ('... and-six ...', I offer, with a smile.
    She shakes her head reprovingly.)

Only Oxford's system of tutorial essays,
     researched, set down and
tendered, criticised, defended, gives the student
     resilience
and responsibility, the attitudes and
     values both Town and
Gown require today for real success throughout life's
     experience.

This is Oxford's secret. Practise writing essays –
     ask for feedback.
Formative assessment does more good than formal
     examinations.
Aristotle was right: all kinds of success in
     learning lead back
to performance – practice polished by a tutor's
     strict observations.

    ('Unless I do it by myself,
    I'll never learn to count, you see.')

WILLIAM MORRIS'S BICYCLE SHOP

The City of Venice and the Island of Sark,
the towpath by the Thames or the Oxford Canal,
each have three characteristics in common:
  an unfailing power to please,
    water, no cars.

Oxford's policy of Park and Ride
discourages visiting motorists from venturing
across the Ring Road in their private cars.
  The City's best viewed on foot,
    or bus, or bike.

This is the site of the old bicycle shop
where the young William Morris began
his remarkable career as a mechanical engineer –
  who soon switched his attention
    from bikes to cars.

Now Oxford has grown to rival Coventry,
another cathedral city that worships motor-cars.
Lord Nuffield's legacy can be seen in Cowley,
  or the College that bears his name,
    or all these cars.

The culture of the private car has prevailed
the world over: no one questions
or challenges the monopoly of the motorist, except
  for those few who are pleased to walk
    beside water.

TECHNOLOGY

Progress always comes at a price.
Modern technology's a mixed blessing
(when it's not an unmitigated curse –
      like motor bikes
         or Twitter).

The mobile phone or e-mail, for example,
increase connectiveness all right,
but cruelly reduce the time
      for serious reflection,
         or real work.

The seductive products of Oxford's
new Technology Park
present an interesting challenge,
      like hand guns,
         or boob jobs:

whether, on balance, they are worth it?
Visit the Museum of the History of Science
to study inventions of real value –
      like writing,
         or the wheel.

BLACKWELL'S BOOKSHOP

Oxford is a City of books,
abounding in authors and publishers,
bookshops, libraries and readers:
philosophers, poets and scientists;
the Oxford University Press;
Blackwell's and the Bodleian Library;
        you and me.

Apart from The Bible, the best
example of an Oxford book
is the Oxford English Dictionary –
now no longer available
as a book. Read it on line.
IT has made volumes redundant for
        you and me.

(But not, as yet, this one!)
Change is always a challenge.
Progress perplexes, as it unfolds.
Spelling reform will be next,
making these words incomprehensible, 2
        u n mi.

CHARITY

'Who is my neighbour?'
Luke, x, 29.

The family's a gift. We choose our friends.
By chance, or mischance, casual neighbours meet,
 exchange some platitudes, a practised smile,
across a garden wall or in the street.

Our neighbour is the one we come across
in daily life: the stranger on the train,
the beggar in the road, a tourist lost,
a frightened child, someone in grief or pain.

We pass them often – at our peril pass
them by – for happiness is found in care,
freely conferred. There is no finer role –
and neighbours crowd around us everywhere.

Consider Oxfam, visit Helen House,
Family Links, Samaritans ... and see
communities of people practising
kindness. Oxford's a source of charity.

In cherishing our neighbour we may find
a way to nourish our own lives – be wise –
serve others – help ourselves – each day. The Good
Samaritan is smiling when he dies.

Samaritans are selfish, I suppose,
at one remove – the best that humans do.
True altruism is unknown. But still,
this selfless selfishness is kind, and true.

Mind you, I wonder how he felt that day,
the one they'd mugged and left half-dead – when some
lowlife* bent down with comfort, kindness, care
to rescue him. Who was it he called 'scum'?

* *Samaritans were the under-class of Judaea.*

THE JAM FACTORY

                    Is
Oxford Marmalade no longer made here?
What's the use of a Jam Factory that
makes no jam? It fails to fit its purpose.
Oxford Station still provides a service.
Business is the business of the Business
School. The traffic in St. Frideswide's Square moves
slowly, but it moves. Things function here. Things
work. They have a purpose. They are useful.
Usefulness is everything. Or is it?
What's the use of poetry, I wonder –
thinking of the Grecian Urn and rinsing
this plain, empty honey-jar, screw-capped and
useful for next season's marmalade (new
Seville oranges, and lemons, water,
sugar, boiled together till they thicken).
Beauty is not truth: it's usefulness, I
claim. Or rather, fitness for the purpose
is true beauty. So, what's the use of
poetry? I know the usual answers:
for instruction and delight. They're wrong, or
insufficient (and I need more useful
pots to hold a year's supply of breakfast
marmalade), for poems have no purpose,
and no uses – just existence. Poetry
                    is.

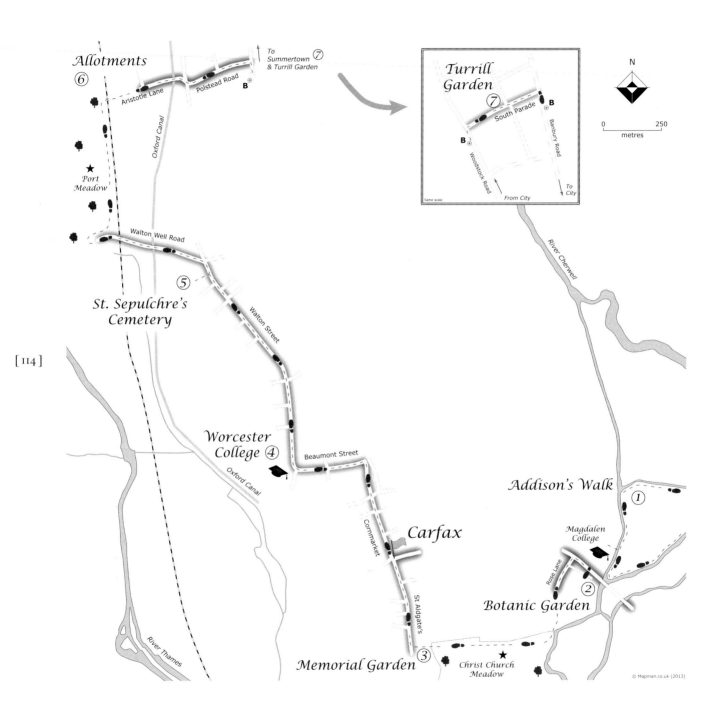

Allotments
⑥

To
Summertown
& Turrill Garden ⑦

Aristotle Lane

Polstead Road   B ⊛

Oxford Canal

Port
Meadow

Walton Well Road

⑤

St. Sepulchre's
Cemetery

Walton Street

Worcester
College ④

Beaumont Street

Oxford Canal

Cornmarket

Carfax

St Aldgate's

Memorial Garden   ③

Christ Church
Meadow

River Thames

Addison's Walk

①

Magdalen
College

Rose Lane

②

Botanic Garden

River Cherwell

Turrill
Garden
⑦

South Parade   B ⊛

B ⊛

Banbury Road

Woodstock Road

To
City

From City

Same scale

N

0   250
metres

[114]

© Mapman.co.uk (2013)

7. SEVEN GARDENS OF OXFORD

WE HAVE CHOSEN – from the many lovely gardens in Oxford – seven we particularly cherish. Each has a story to tell.

The walk begins in Magdalen College at the east end of the High Street. ADDISON'S WALK is found behind the older college buildings close to the Deer Park.

Cross the road after leaving Magdalen to visit the BOTANIC GARDENS.

Then walk down Rose Lane along the western side of these gardens and cross Christ Church Meadow to find the MEMORIAL GARDEN on the far western side.

From here, walk up St. Aldate's to Carfax. Continue along the Cornmarket and Magdalen Street; then turn left down Beaumont Street, at the end of which you will come to WORCESTER COLLEGE and its extensive and lovely GARDEN.

Leave Worcester College and walk northwards along Walton Street. Near the end, almost opposite the turning (right) to St. Bernard's Road, lies ST. SEPULCHRE'S CEMETERY.

Now return to Walton Street, continue briefly northwards before turning left into Walton Well Road. Cross the canal and railway. ALLOTMENTS BY THE RAILWAY can be seen from the bridge. You can find others by taking the old dust-cart track that runs northward through Port Meadow. This connects to a path leading back (eastwards) into Oxford across the railway, ultimately joining Aristotle Lane. Here are more ALLOTMENTS.

Continue to the end of Aristotle Lane, cross Mayfield Road and walk eastwards along Polstead Road. Here you can take a bus northwards to Summertown. Walk along South Parade to find the TURRILL SCULPTURE GARDEN concealed behind the Public Library.

Return to Oxford by continuing to the end of South Parade and the Banbury Road, where you will be able to catch a bus back to the centre of the City. The bus stops at the southern end of St. Giles, from where you reach Carfax by walking along the Cornmarket.

ADDISON'S WALK

'A painted meadow, or a purling stream'
(Addison)

He often walked here, where fritillaries,
like pearls and rubies scattered in the grass,
transform this spot in spring. The garden is
one of the glories of the City: pass
the College by, you may, but not this peerless walk.

A Magdalen Fellow, Joseph Addison
was one of those who shaped the modern age,
refining literary taste. No one
did more to shape our culture – on the stage,
through essays and reviews, his published 'table-talk'.

His walk has come full circle since those days,
skirting the river, Magdalen Bridge, the park
where Magdalen's famous deer may safely graze,
to reach the point from where it started. Mark
the changing charms of English landscaped wilderness.

He hated party politics, and wrote
for women readers just as much as men.
Read *Cato*, read the splendid *Ode*, and note
his mastery of the middle style. His pen
prevailed. His varied life was not without success.

Visit this ancient College in the spring:
glance at the Chapel, leave the cloistered quad,
turn right and cross a little bridge – to bring
you to the special Walk his feet once trod.
Tread softly where the snowdrops grow. His spirit's near.

And who may hope for more than modest fame?
I'd rather be remembered for a walk
like this, than any written work. His name
is rarely mentioned now in Oxford. Talk
of Addison is rare: his legacy is here.

The Botanic Garden

Confronting Magdalen College's fine tower,
Oxford's old Physick garden can be found.
Source of ragwort – and healing herbs, this ground
is sacred, dedicated to the flower
and fruit of Botany. Devote an hour
or two of study here, while strolling round
the formal gardens. Look and learn. The sound
of birdsong, scent of blooms make this a bower
of bliss for Oxford's visitors. But wait!
First pause by beds of roses, rife
with colour. Search for the inscribed stone here,
where penicillin's pioneers appear.
Grateful survivors should commemorate
the names of those, now dead, who saved their life.

THE MEMORIAL GARDEN

I think continually of those who died in battle
amidst the screams of shells and wounded men,
sitting alone, in sunlight, in this quiet garden,
who never saw the sun, or home, again.

They were cold, frightened, unprepared for death, bewildered –
I love this peaceful place, its flowers, its trees –
in all that cruel mud and wire, the blood, the gunfire ...
birdsong and this still pool, this gentle breeze.

I wonder if they thought about the Alice garden
crouched in a crater, waiting for their death,
where the White Rabbit led her down its magic burrow,
crying for Wonderland with their last breath.

WORCESTER COLLEGE GARDEN

So, what are gardens for, I wonder, while
the autumn leaves fall softly on the lake?
Gardens make work for gardeners: I smile
to see them busy with the broom, the hoe, the rake.

Gardens are restful. Sit and watch the lake –
shadows and sunlight, ripples that delete
the perfectly-reflected trees to make
another picture that is never quite complete.

Designers, painters, poets – all come here.
A garden makes a seed-bed for the arts.
I hear a distant echo – faint, but clear –
of summer's music by the lake. A figure darts

across the water, long-remembered, Puck
performing in another summer's *Dream*
so long ago ... a solitary duck
demands attention, landing near the lake's extreme.

Some gardens will change lives, renew our hope
and help us learn that all may yet be well.
Dead leaves regenerate; still lakes give scope
for possibilities no rain-cloud can dispel.

ST. SEPULCHRE'S CEMETERY

Words borrowed often change their sound and sense
and grammar strangely: Latin *sanctus* sounds
unlike our *saint:* meant 'holy', not 'someone
who's canonised'; and was an adjective,
while English *saint*'s a noun. Loanwords transform their function.

The chapel – of the Holy Sepulchre –
is gone, transformed from stone to memory,
leaving the churchyard to the butterflies,
the brambles and the beasts – rabbit and fox,
addict and derelict – a fragile ecosystem.

A band of volunteers comes here to work
to make a garden from a wilderness,
transform this quiet place for all to see,
revealing long-lost gravestones, hidden paths,
space for children to play and elders rest together –

where artists come to paint the tranquil scene
and poets pen their verses, and transform
this transient view to something that might last
a little longer – artistry. For art
offers the best hope of postponing our extinction.

THE ALLOTMENTS BY THE RAILWAY

Watch them from the train:
old men tending bonfires
on their neat allotments,
   munching apples
   in the pungent smoke.

The wife has sent them out –
to clear the house for cleaning.
'I married him,' she thinks,
   'for better or worse,
   but not for lunch.'

He grumbles and complies –
each attentive to their task,
transforming dust and debris
   to fiery ash,
   and shining surface.

Admire the rough tenderness
of these settled marriages –
miracles of faithfulness
   from unlikely partners
   reconciled by time.

Until one day you look up
from the recalcitrant flames
to see a train pass by,
   and realise the passengers
   are watching you.

THE TURRILL SCULPTURE GARDEN

Sculpture looks comfortable in this quiet garden.
These bronze leaves seem to leap and pirouette –
leaf-faces grin and grimace here –
amongst the litter autumn leaves outside
the library, where wisdom and silence
hold readers still as statues, as they slowly
turn the leaves, and learn. The leaves are turning
autumn-yellow, orange-red, bronze,
in this quiet garden graced by sculpture.

ENVOI: TRANSIENCE

Crossing the bridge, as I walk to the station,
I glance down at the river flowing past,
silent and dark – and unremarkable.
From source to sea the Thames never runs fast,
nor fails to run. It flows without cessation.

For more than fifty years I've come this way
along Hythe Bridge Street, past the old canal
basin – a car-park now – across the bridge
to Blackwell's modern building, which I shall
not live to see razed and replaced one day,

through the new square by the old L.M.S.
station-site – now the Said Business School.
This side of Oxford nothing stays the same.
And yet the eternal river proves the rule:
though all things change, rivers and hills change less.

But even hills and rivers change in time.
Once, long ago, this region was a lake
until the water smashed the Goring Gap,
a tidal wave of change that helped to make
the gentle Thames of Spenser's matchless rhyme.

And far into the future, one hot day,
the river will dry up and disappear
beneath the fierce glare of the swelling sun.
Change is the only constant feature here.
Hills crumble, rivers vanish, things decay.

ACKNOWLEDGEMENTS

The authors and publishers would like to acknowledge the assistance of the following in the creation of the paintings in this book:

Addison Walk, with kind permission of Magdalen College, Oxford

The Alfred Jewel at the Ashmolean Museum, Oxford

Blackwell Bookshop, Oxford

Blenheim Palace, Woodstock

The Bodleian Library, University of Oxford

The Department of Earth Sciences, University of Oxford

Dorchester Abbey

Examination Schools, University of Oxford

Headington Hill Hall, with kind permission of Oxford Brookes University

The Jam Factory, Oxford

Keble College Chapel, with kind permission of Keble College, Oxford

Kelmscott Manor, Lechlade

Le Manoir aux Quat'Saisons

Museum of the History of Science, Oxford

New College Chapel, with kind permission of New College, Oxford

Oxfam Bookshop, St. Giles, Oxford

Oxford Botanic Gardens

Oxford Castle view, with kind permission of Malmaison Hotel, Oxford

Oxford Town Hall, with kind permission of the Oxford City Council

The Sheldonian Theatre, Oxford

The Shelley Memorial, with kind permission of University College, Oxford

St. Mary the Virgin Church, Iffley

St. Michael at the Northgate Church

St. Sepulchre's Cemetery, Oxford

The Turrill Sculpture Garden, Summertown, Oxford

The University Museum, Oxford

War Memorial Gardens, Christ Church, Oxford

Worcester College, Oxford